Hum Chan, Iwan Zahar

Maximizing Learning Outcomes by Socratic Questioning: Exploring the Pedagogical Applications and Challenges among Language Lecturers at Universiti Malaysia Kelantan

Der GRIN Verlag publiziert seit 1998 wissenschaftliche Arbeiten von Studenten, Hochschul-
lehrern und anderen Akademikern als eBook und gedrucktes Buch. Die Verlagswebsite
www.grin.com ist die ideale Plattform zur Veröffentlichung von Hausarbeiten, Abschlussar-
beiten, wissenschaftlichen Aufsätzen, Dissertationen und Fachbüchern.

Document Nr. V208743

Hum Chan, Iwan Zahar

Maximizing Learning Outcomes by Socratic Questioning: Exploring the Pedagogical Applications and Challenges among Language Lecturers at Universiti Malaysia Kelantan

GRIN Verlag

Die Deutsche Bibliothek verzeichnet diese Publikation in der Deutschen Nationalbibliografie; detaillierte bibliografische Daten sind im Internet über http://dnb.d-nb.de/ abrufbar.

1. Auflage 2013
Copyright © 2013 GRIN Verlag GmbH
http://www.grin.com
Druck und Bindung: Books on Demand GmbH, Norderstedt Germany
ISBN 978-3-656-36337-8

Maximizing Learning Outcomes by Socratic Questioning: Exploring the Pedagogical Applications and Challenges among Language Lecturers at Universiti Malaysia Kelantan

Hum Chan, Iwan Zahar

Universiti Malaysia Kelantan

Abstract: This study aims to explore the perception of language lecturers toward the pedagogical applications and challenges of Socrates Questioning for language teaching. Quantitative method with questionnaire was applied to collect data from 20 language lecturers at Universiti Malaysia Kelantan (UMK). Data was analyzed by SPSS. The findings revealed that applying Socrates questioning in language teaching can enhance teaching effectiveness, affect students' learning behaviour and promote students' learning activities that can produce optimal learning outcomes. However, fruitful learning outcomes depended on lecturers' ability and skills to apply questions in pedagogical manner linking Socrates questions and questioning techniques regarding the target language, teaching procedures and learning activities that can enrich profound outcomes.

Keywords: Learning Outcomes, Pedagogical Application, Socrates Questions

INTRODUCTION

In general, effective questioning by teachers can give significant effect on students' learning and learning outcomes (Orland 2001). From the evolution of Socrates point of view, better questioning can effectively transfer knowledge to students. On average, teachers ask nearly 400 questions per day or at least1.000 questions per week. The purpose of questioning ranges from drawing students' attention and participation, checking their understanding, evaluating learning outcomes, provoking discussion, revising teaching contents and enhancing critical thinking (Orland 2001). In the process, teachers use varieties of questions, for example, Yes/No questions, Open-ended questions, Convergent questions, and divergent questions (Gabrielatos 1997; Chaudron 1988); display questions (Ellis 1994) or inferential questions (Lam 2011) and among other questions.

However, researchers criticized that most teachers apply these questions for basic level of cognitive learning lacked driver to link teaching contents and procedures to reach maximum outcomes since teachers do not have clear focus in asking questions (Suter 2001). Paul and Elder (2005) also gave similar comment that poor questioning technique cannot produce deeper understanding of students that can develop students' rationale, judgement, and understanding. Effective questioning by teachers can also reduce teacher talking time

(TTT), provoke students' participation and manage teaching time effectiveness (Gabrielatos 1997). To do so, teachers must possess expertise in mastering high-level cognitive questions such as Socrates questioning.

Socrates uses questions to provoke students' attention, make them listen to lectures, analyze concepts, and develop critical mind (Cotton 1988; Orland 2001). Today, the application has remained an orthodox for language teaching. However, most teachers still go wide in applying Socrates techniques as they are not able design systematic and precise questions to gain explicit and depth responses from students (Norman & Patnode 2002). Unclear responses from students to the target language can reflect weakness of teaching and poor questioning skills. Therefore, this study intends to explore the perceptions among language lecturers at Universiti Malaysia Kelantan toward the pedagogical applications and challenges of Socrates Questioning on maximizing students' learning outcomes.

LITERATURE REVIEW

Applications of Socrates Questions

Socrates is well known ancient Greek philosopher who has never written anything. He is also known for his questioning strategy. Is he really had questioning strategy so called elenchus? In modern times, elenchus become a proper name. The most important activity in elenchus is search. In Greek works, elenchus can be used to mean "refutation", "testing", "censure" and "reproach". Socrate's procedure will be as follows; When the interlocutor asserts a thesis p, Socrates considers false and secure agreement to propose q and r. Socrates argues and the interlocutor agrees that q and r entail not-p. Socrates then claim that not-p is true, and p false (Vlatos, 1994). However Many scholars is against Vlatos'opinion about "socratec" methods because Plato and Socates himself had never name it. It is not clear whether the elenchus is a process (which means to cross-examine, to put to test, to put to the proof or to indicate), or a result (which could mean to shame, to refute or to prove) Scoot, 2001.

However, Paul and Elder select Socrates questions and place them in hierarchically starts from; clarity, accuracy, precision, relevance, depth, breath and significance. Some scholars has already selected Socrates questions and they are applying several referential questions, convergent and divergent questions (Gabrielatos 1997; Chaudron 1988). Undeniable these questions are stimulus and meaningful, but in the postmodern language teaching and learning lecturers need to master high order questioning to promote high level cognitive thinking. To this end, Paul and Elder (2005) suggested teachers applying Socrates Questions to provoke students' involvement, attention and critical thinking which help fostering deeper understanding. In this regard, Socrates posed questions about the subject matters, while students explore answers and extend the discussion (Orland, 2001). According to Paul and Elder (2005), Socrates Questions are applied for the following purposes:

Table 1

Socrates Questions and Pedagogical Implications

Example of Questions	Pedagogical Application
Could you give us an example? Could you explain further?	Questions for clarification
Why this word is important? Why do you think that?	Question about initial question or issue
Why would someone make this assumption? What could we assume instead?	Question for assumption
What would be an example? Why do you think this is right?	Question for reason and evidence
Where did you get that idea? What caused you to feel that way?	Question for origin or source
What effect would that have? What is an alternative?	Question for implication or consequence
How would other groups of people respond this question? Why?	Question for opinion

(Source: Richard Paul & Linda Elder 2005)

As displayed in the table, Socrates Questioning aims to develop learning outcomes through seven pedagogical applications. First question is used for clarification, second for initial question or issue, third for assumption, fourth for reason and evidence, fifth for origin or source, sixth for implication or consequence, and seventh for opinion. Therefore, researchers such as Paul and Elder (2005) recommended that Socrates questioning is effective and stimulus in fostering students' learning outcomes since it helps activate the process of thinking and transform the process throughout learning to develop cognitive, affective and meta-cognitive domain.

Outcome-Based Teaching and Learning

Biggs and Tang (2007) define Outcome-Based Teaching and Learning (OBTL) as a process of transferring the target contents through applying rigorous method and rubric assessment to evaluate teaching demonstration and learning outcomes. In general, OBTL comprises of three models: what the student is; what the teacher does, and what the student does (Biggs & Tang 2007). The first two models are used to enhance knowledge, concept and understanding to students at elementary and pre-intermediate level. The method is mainly focused on teacher-centred with controlling management. The two levels are not compatible to apply for higher education which is implied by technology and questioning skills that is required the third level. The third level is a student-centred model that requires independent learning to explore the intended outcome beyond information, conception and understanding. This model aims to enhance students' different levels of knowledge through stipulating desired learning outcomes to the target contents, and enhancing level of understanding through effective teaching and learning techniques (Biggs & Tang 2007). In the postmodern pedagogy, outcome-based teaching and learning has been widely applied especially in higher education.

3

Many researchers claimed that questioning plays most important part of teaching. Therefore, many scholars have developed different questioning approaches. For example, Adam (2009) introduced QDAR Model (Q = Questions, D = Decision, A= Action, R= Result and Reflection) to show the correlation between teaching, learning and result.

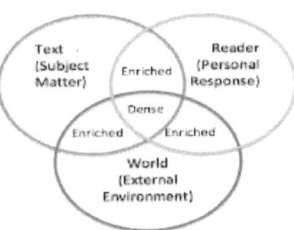

$$Q \rightarrow D \rightarrow A \rightarrow R$$

Questions → Decisions → Actions → Results (reflection)

Figure 1: QDAR Model (Adam, 2009)

Adam extended the explanation that this imperative process can help teachers as well as learners to construct their understanding and learning outcomes, especially questions can pave the way to achieve an intended outcome through signifying, remodelling and reconceptualising and solving problem of the target contents. However, QDAR Model was mainly introduced as a vehicle for action learning in business domain.

Another questioning approach was suggested by Christenbury and Kelly (1983) that comprises of three components (1) the Subject Matter—the target language, contents or topic to be discussed, (2) the Student's Behaviour – how students give responses to the subject matters, and (3) the Classroom Environment– the overall view of subject matter to students. Applying all the components in teaching can transfer knowledge to students through interactive response.

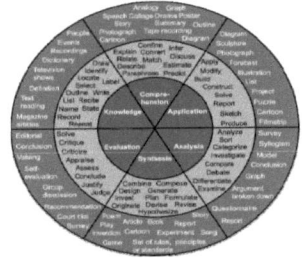

Figure 2: Questioning Circle (Christenbury & Kelly 1983)

However, the postmodern pedagogy for language teaching requires teachers to apply systematic and high order thinking question such as Socrates to engage teaching contents and learning activities. The application aims to enhance an ultimate outcome through promoting critical thinking in Bloom's Taxonomy. This method can promote students' learning beyond memorized-based technique that demanded students to develop reasoning and element of thoughts through mental process (Paul, 1985). In Bloom, teachers use questions to enhance knowledge through developing high order thinking.

For example, teacher might ask *"What is past simple?"* to cultivate students' knowledge; "When do we use past simple?" to check students' comprehension; "Is it right if someone say "he goes to market yesterday"?" to focus students' application; "what is wrong with the statement "he goes to market yesterday?" to develop students' analysis; "Can you compare the differences between the sentences "I went to market yesterday and I have been to the market twice?" to develop students 'synthesis; and " Why is it wrong to say " I have been to market yesterday?" for evaluation (Paul & Elder 2005).

Figure 3: Bloom's Taxonomy & Questions

4

METHODS AND MATERIALS

Quantitative method was employed with questionnaire. The questionnaire was designed in two Parts: Description of Respondents and Application and challenges of Socrates Questions. 20 questionnaires were distributed to language lecturers in Centre for Language Studies and Generic Development at Universiti Malaysia Kelanta (UMK). The language lecturers were randomly selected among full-time staff who teach different languages, for example, English, Khmer, Chinese, Japanese, German, Thai, Arabic and Malay.

Table 2

Number of Language Lecturers

Language Lecturers	Number
English	8
Japanese	1
German	3
Chinese	3
Malay	1
Cambodian	1
Thai	2
Arabic	1
Total	20

Data was analyzed by SPSS to compare the frequencies and percentage. The comparison was made to find out the significant different pedagogical applications and challenges among language lecturers who employ questions during their teaching to enhance students learning outcomes.

RESULTS AND DISCUSSION

Description of Respondents

The result indicated that 45 % of the selected lecturers teach English, 15 % teach German, 10% teach Chinese and Cambodian, and 5% teach Japanese, Thai, Malay and Arabic Language. The results further revealed that 40% of lecturers teach elementary, 35 % intermediate, 5% upper-intermediate and 20% teach all levels. 40% of the selected lecturers spent over 15 hours, 30% used 12-15 hours and 10% spent below 6 hours for teaching a week. 55% of lecturers designed lesson into three stages (pre-, while and post teaching), 25% designed into two stages (pre-and post teaching), 10% designed four stages (pre-, transitional teaching, while and post teaching). Lecturers gave several reasons to design lessons into three stages, for example, to draw students' attention and interests in pre-teaching, easy to demonstrate teaching and organizing classroom activities, and creating interactive steps to engage teaching contents, learning activities and learning outputs.

The result also revealed that lecturers used all types of questions during teaching, but the frequency of questioning is different in each teaching stage. On average, lecturers asked

5

5-10 questions per hours, especially during the while teaching. In general, they used open-ended questions to explore detailed responses from students. The main purpose of questioning by lecturers was to keep students focus and interests, to create communication in classes, to make students think and to make their teaching effective.

Pedagogical Application of Socrates Questions in Teaching

Pre-Teaching

The result showed that lecturers tended to frequently ask questions for clarification and opinion during the pre-teaching. 45% of lecturers used questions for clarification, while 30% asked students about opinion. Only 15%-20% of lecturers used questions for initial and issue, assumption, evidence and origin in the beginning stage of teaching. The data further revealed that the least frequently used questions were questions for evidence and origin. Lecturers claimed that the common purpose of questioning was to identify students' knowledge and understanding to the topic to be discussed, to provoke students' curiosity, and to explore students' opinion and expose students to the target contents.

While Teaching

The result indicated that the most frequently asked questions during the while teaching were not different from those questions used in the pre-teaching stage. 35% of the selected lecturers asked students to clarify the answer and 40% of them ask students to give their opinions. However, the least frequently used questions in this teaching stage were questions for origin, implications, or consequence. The common reasons that lectures asked questions for clarification and opinion to students were to check students' abilities to utilize the target language, to encourage them in discussion on the subject matter, to provoke interactive learning activities, and to evaluate students' comprehension.

Post Teaching

The data did not revealed different questions used during the post teaching stage. It indicated that 55% of lecturers asked students to make clarification, while 35% of them explored student's opinions. This stage, lecturers rarely asked questions for assumptions, origin or evidence. The results further highlighted that the purpose of asking questions during this stage was to check students' comprehension, opinions and information about the instruction.

Challenges in applying questions in classrooms

It was found that 70% of lecturers preferred oral questioning technique due to its effectiveness, convenience and easiness under time constraints. Lectures further claimed that oral questioning technique was to develop students' speaking and reasoning skills. The result also indicated that 25% of lectures employed all types of questioning techniques to improve

students' four macro-skills such as listening, speaking, reading and writing. In general, the result revealed that 50% of lecturers frequently asked questions to individual, 45% whole class and 30% group and pairs. However, the results indicated several challenges to language lecturers in applying questions in classrooms. The common challenges revealed by the study related to student's language proficiency, vocabulary, self-confidence, and motivation to talk. The literature review regarding language teaching, learning, and questioning highlighted that Socrates Questions played a central role in producing learning outcomes. As mentioned by Paul and Elder (2005), language teachers used questions to assign tasks, express problems and delineate issues in teaching and learning. Beyond this, teachers used questions to grab students' involvement and interests, to check their comprehension and knowledge, to review teaching contents, to promote critical thinking (Orland, 2001), to arouse curiosity, passion and intellectual habits (Lam, 2011), and generate language proficiency and control, guide, and encourage students to learn the target language (Suter 2001).

Similar implication was indicated by this study. Language lecturers utilized, if not all, at least 5-10 questions per hours during teaching. The most frequently asked questions were the open-ended questions to gain clarification and opinion from students on the subject matter. Questions were used in a range of purposes in different teaching stage. In the pre-teaching lecturers used questions to identify students' knowledge and understanding to the topic to be discussed, to arouse students' curiosity, and to explore students' opinion on the target contents. During while teaching lecturers asked questions to measure students' abilities in utilizing the target language, to encourage them in discussing the subject matter, to provoke learning activities, and to evaluate their comprehension. The final stage of teaching lecturers used questions to evaluate students' language acquisition and reflect of the instruction. Due to time constraints, lecturers used oral questioning technique to individual and whole class.

However, the results revealed that lecturers could not used all types of Socrates Questions, for example, questions for assumptions, evidence, origins and implications in teaching due to an unfamiliarity and low language proficiency of students. The unfamiliarity occurred from both lecturers and students. Lecturers lacked awareness of fostering questioning effectiveness in teaching and learning activities. The evidence was crystal clear that lecturers did not give definite reason they use questions for "pre-, while and post teaching. Many lecturers responded with "no ideas or no comments". Other lecturers complained that students had low vocabulary that they could not build meaningful sentences to answer the questions. For this reason, they feel shy and unconfident to give responses.

Other lecturers asserted that the students were quite passive and unresponsive to questions due to their habits. When asked questions, they just gave smile and keep quiet.

CONCLUSION

In short, this study aims to explore the perceptions among language lecturers at University Malaysia Kelantan toward the pedagogical implications and challenges of Socrates Questioning in teaching language. Lecturers used at least 5-10 questions during teaching for different purposes, for example, identifying students' knowledge and understanding, arousing the curiosity, exploring the opinions, measuring learning outcomes, fostering classroom involvement, and evaluating teaching effectiveness. The common pedagogical application employed by lecturers at UMK is an oral questioning technique due to time constraints, numbers of students, and questioning effectiveness.

However, there are three factors challenging lecturers in applying Socrates Questioning in language teaching at Universiti Malaysia Kelantan. First, it resulted in teacher's background. Some lecturers are not familiar with Socrates Questions so they cannot apply them rightly and effectively. Second, it related to student's language proficiency. To give meaningful responses to the questions, students need possess a large amount of vocabulary. This problem was also concerned with learning environment lacking motivation to make students critical thinking and giving response to questions. Third, it concerned with time constraints and numbers of students in the class. Lecturers cannot shift different questioning techniques, for example, individual questioning, pair questioning and group questioning that provoke students' involvement and interests to the intended contents.

The findings from the study suggested language lecturers at UMK reflecting upon their questions and questioning techniques. Lecturers should design and apply effective questions such as Socrates to create teaching efficiency and produce fruitful learning outcomes. To this end, lecturers should frequently apply Socrates Questions in their teaching. All in all, this study has given ideal suggestion to language lecturers in preparing and applying Socrates Questions to foster students learning outcomes. Therefore, further study with larger participants and locations would give greater benefits.

REFERENCES

Adam, M (2010) *Action Learning and Its Applications, Present and Future.* Boshyk, Y., & Dilworth, L. (Eds.) Palgrave Macmillan Publishers.

Biggs, J., & Tang, C. (2007). *Teaching for Quality of Learning at University* .Open University Press. New York: McGraw Hill

Chaudron, C. (1988). Second language classrooms: Research on teaching and learning. Cambridge: Cambridge University Press.

Cotton, K. (1988). *Classroom Questioning.* North West Regional Educational Laboratory.

Ellis, R. (1994). *The study of second language acquisition.* Oxford: Oxford University Press

Gabrielatos, C. (1997). A question of function: Teacher questions in the EFL classroom. *Paper given at 18 th eAnnual TESOL Greece Convention,* National Bank of Greece Training Centre, Glyfada, Greece, 12-13 April 1997.

Lam, F (2011) The Socratic Method as an Approach to L earning and Its Benefits. *Dietrich College Honors Theses.* Paper 134. Retrieved 15 dec from http://repositor y.cmu .edu/hsshonor s/134.

Norman, M., & Patnode, H. (2002). *Socrates Method: Leverage Questions to Increase the Performance.* Program Management and Leadership. United States.

Paul, R. (1985). Bloom's Taxonomy and Critical Instruction. *Educational Leadership.* Vol. 42, pp. 36

Paul, R., & Elder, L. (2005). *The Miniature Guide to the Art of Asking Essential Questions* . Retrieved from Foundation for Critical Thinking. www.criticalthingking.org

Paul, R., & Elder, L. (2008). Critical Thinking: The Arts of Socrates Questioning, Part III. *Journal of Development Education,* 31(3), 34-35.

Scott, G. A. (2002) *Does Socrates have a method. Rethinking elephensus.* Pensylvania : Pensylvania State University Press

Suter, C. (2001). *Exploring Teachers' Questions and Feedbacks.* University of Birmingham.

Vlatos, G. (1994). *Socratic Studies.* Cambridge:Cambridge University Press